Sickle Cell Disease

Carol Baldwin

Heinemann Library
Chicago, Illinois

Customer Service 888-454-2279

Visit our website at www.heinemannlibrary.com

Designed by Patricia Stevenson
Printed and bound in the United States
by Lake Book Manufacturing

07 06 05 04 03
10 9 8 7 6 5 4 3 2 1

Library of Congress Cataloging-in-Publication Data
Baldwin, Carol, 1943–
    Sickle cell disease / Carol Baldwin.
        p. cm. — (Health matters)
Includes bibliographical references and index.
    ISBN 1-40340-252-3
    1. Sickle cell anemia—Juvenile literature.
    [1. Sickle cell anemia. 2. Diseases.] I. Title.

RC641.7.S5 B345 2002
616.1'527—dc21
                                        2001007975

Acknowledgments
The author and publishers are grateful to the
following for permission to reproduce copyright
material:

Cover photograph by Paul Epley/Picturesque/
PictureQuest

p. 4 Oliver Meckes/Ottawa/Photo Researchers, Inc.;
p. 5 David Brooks/Corbis Stock Market; p. 6 June
Hill Pedigo/Custom Medical Stock Photo, Inc.; p. 7
David Woodroffe; p. 8 Stephen Agricola/Stock
Boston, Inc./PictureQuest; p. 9 Joe Sohm/Stock
Connection/PictureQuest; pp. 10, 12, 22 Trevor
Clifford/Heinemann Library; p. 11 Gary
Hansen/PhotoTake; p. 13 Tom McCarthy/Photo
Network/PictureQuest; pp. 14, 23 Maggy Milner; p.
15 David Young-Wolff/PhotoEdit/PictureQuest; pp.
16, 21 Andrew M. Levine/Photo Researchers, Inc.;
p. 17 Eyewire/Getty Images; p. 18 James
Shaffer/PhotoEdit; p. 19 Don Stevenson/Index Stock
Imagery/PictureQuest; p. 20 Will and Deni
McIntyre/Photo Researchers, Inc.; p. 24 David
Young-Wolff/PhotoEdit; p. 25 Frank Simonetti/Stock
Connection/PictureQuest; p. 26 Sickle Cell Disease
Association of America; p. 27T Zuma
Press/Newscom; p. 27B AP Wide World Photos

Every effort has been made to contact copyright
holders of any material reproduced in this book.
Any omissions will be rectified in subsequent
printings if notice is given to the publisher.

Some words are shown in bold, **like this.** You can find out what they
mean by looking in the glossary.

Contents

What Is Sickle Cell Disease?

Sickle cell disease is a **condition** that affects a person's blood. Blood is made of different kinds of **cells. Red blood cells** are one type of blood cell. Normal red blood cells are round and flexible. But sickle cells are different. They are red blood cells that are stiff and have a curved shape. These cells are named after old-fashioned farm tools called sickles that are used to cut wheat. In people who have sickle cell disease, some of their red blood cells become stiff and curved, or sickled.

Blood travels through your body in small tubes called **blood vessels.** As your blood moves, it's the red blood cells' job to carry oxygen to all parts of your body. Your body's cells need oxygen to do their jobs and stay healthy.

Normal red blood cells are round and soft. Instead of being flexible, sickle cells are stiffer and curved in shape.

How does sickle cell disease affect people?

Because of their shape, sickle cells don't live as long as normal red blood cells do. They also can't move as freely through the blood vessels. They can get stuck in blood vessels and block blood flow to parts of the body. When blood flow is cut off to a part of the body, people with sickle cell disease have **symptoms** such as tiredness, pain, and swelling in that body part. Sickle cell disease also makes people more likely to get **infections.**

Sickle cell disease can cause a friend to tire more easily than you do.

Sickle cell disease affects people in different ways. Some people hardly know they have it. They might have only one or two instances of mild pain a year. And the pain might only last for a few minutes. Other people have a lot of pain that can last for several days, and they might have this pain more often. They sometimes have to miss school or work because of it.

What Causes Sickle Cell Disease?

One set of blood vessels (shown in bright red) carries red blood cells full of oxygen from the lungs. As they travel through your body, the cells release oxygen where it is needed. Another set of blood vessels (shown in dark red) carries the blood cells back to the lungs to pick up more oxygen.

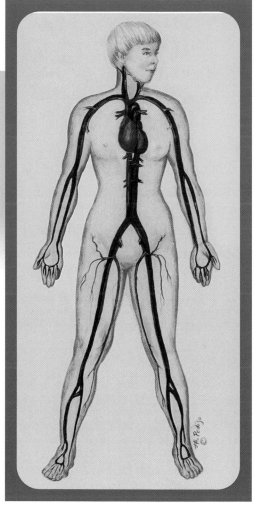

The job of red blood cells

To understand sickle cell disease, you first need to know a little more about what your blood does. When you breathe, air goes into your body through your nose and mouth. It then travels to your lungs. Your heart is a special muscle that pumps blood through your **blood vessels** all around your body. As blood passes through the blood vessels in your lungs, your **red blood cells** pick up oxygen from the air in your lungs.

Your red blood cells then carry the oxygen to all of the other **cells** in your body as they travel. Your body is made of millions of tiny living cells. These cells need oxygen to live, grow, and repair themselves.

How red blood cells carry oxygen

Red blood cells contain a substance called **hemoglobin.**
Think of hemoglobin as a bus and oxygen as the passengers.
Like a bus, hemoglobin picks up oxygen, carries it around
the body, and drops it off in your body's cells where it is
needed. When hemoglobin in normal red blood cells releases
oxygen, the cells stay the same shape. But, in people with
sickle cell disease, the red blood cells become curved and stiff
when the oxygen is released.

Sickle-shaped blood cells have trouble passing through the
body's smaller blood vessels. Sometimes they get stuck and
plug up the blood vessel. This stops blood from reaching that
particular part of the body. This means that part of the body
doesn't get oxygen, and that can cause a lot of pain.

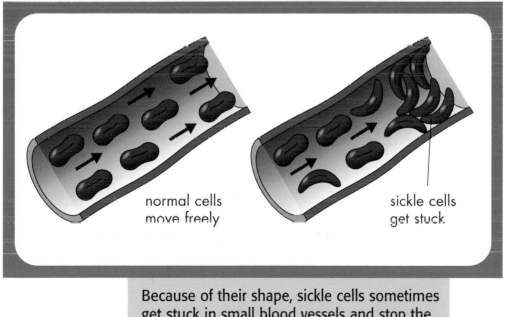

normal cells
move freely

sickle cells
get stuck

Because of their shape, sickle cells sometimes
get stuck in small blood vessels and stop the
blood from flowing normally. Because blood
travels all around the body, this can happen
almost anywhere.

How does a person get sickle cell disease?

Sickle cell disease is an **inherited** disease. That means you can't "catch" sickle cell disease like you can catch a cold. Children are born with the disease when their parents pass along certain **genes** to them.

Every baby is born with one set of genes from the mother and another set from the father. The instructions for building your body are passed down in these genes. Your genes determine all kinds of characteristics, including whether you have curly or straight hair, big or small feet, and light or dark eyes. They even determine the type of blood you have.

Everyone has two copies of the gene for **hemoglobin.** One gene comes from the mother and one comes from the father. A person who receives normal hemoglobin genes from both parents would not have any sickle cell problems. It takes a double dose of sickle cell genes, one from each parent, to produce sickle cell disease.

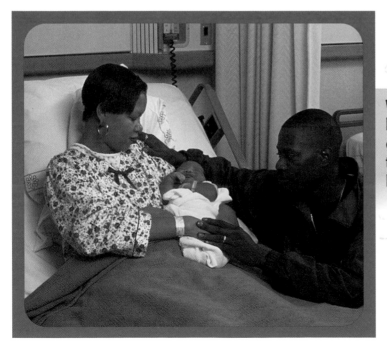

Whether or not a child has sickle cell disease depends on the genes the child inherits from his or her parents.

A child who inherits only one sickle cell gene has what is called **sickle cell trait.** People with sickle cell trait, who have one sickle cell gene and one normal gene, are called **carriers.** They have some sickle cells in their blood, but not many. These people do not have sickle cell disease. But they could pass it on to their own children when they grow up if their partner also has sickle cell trait. If both parents are sickle cell carriers, they could have children with normal hemoglobin, with sickle cell trait, or with sickle cell disease.

Sickle cell disease affects people of some backgrounds more often than others.

Who does sickle cell disease affect?

In the United States, most cases of sickle cell disease occur among African Americans and Hispanics of Caribbean descent. This means that their parents, grandparents, or great-grandparents were born in Africa or a Caribbean country such as Jamaica. About one in every four hundred African Americans has sickle cell disease. But some people whose ancestors came from countries around the Mediterranean Sea, such as Greece, Italy, and Saudi Arabia, can also have sickle cell disease.

Diagnosing Sickle Cell Disease

When **red blood cells** become sickled, a person's body will attack and destroy them. But his or her body can't make new blood cells fast enough to replace them. This can cause a problem called **anemia.** Anemia is one sign that a person has sickle cell disease. Anemia occurs when the body has too few red blood cells. When a person has anemia, he or she gets tired very easily. He or she also gets **infections** more easily than most people. Sometimes the whites of the person's eyes have a yellowish color, known as jaundice. In children under the age of two, sickle cell disease can make their hands and feet swell up and hurt.

Other **symptoms** of sickle cell disease include pains in the arms, legs, hips, and shoulders. Chest and stomach pain, fever, coughing, and problems breathing are also symptoms of sickle cell disease.

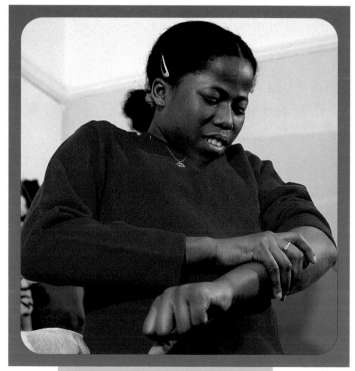

The symptoms of sickle cell disease come and go. Many people with sickle cell disease feel fine most of the time. But, when symptoms do occur, they can be painful.

Testing for sickle cell disease

Doctors perform certain blood tests on a person to find out if they have sickle cell disease. The tests show the doctor the type of **hemoglobin** in the person's red blood cells. To do these tests, the doctor takes a small amount of blood from the person. The first test is called a screening test. It tells whether a person's blood contains sickle hemoglobin or not. But this test can't tell whether a person has **sickle cell trait** or sickle cell disease.

To find out which a person has, another test must be done. In a laboratory, a small amount of the person's blood is treated to make the red blood cells release their hemoglobin. The hemoglobin is placed on a special paper. Then, a tiny electrical charge is passed through the hemoglobin. The electricity makes the hemoglobin move. Sickle hemoglobin moves differently than normal hemoglobin. This test shows the doctor the amount of each kind of hemoglobin in a person's blood. If there is a lot of sickle hemoglobin, the person has sickle cell disease.

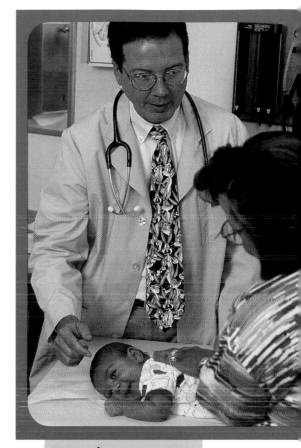

More than 40 states test newborn babies for sickle cell disease.

11

Treating Sickle Cell Disease

Fighting infection

Your spleen is a body part located behind your stomach. It is part of your body's **immune system.** Your immune system protects your body from **infection** by fighting the germs that cause illnesses. When sickle cells block the flow of blood to the spleen, the spleen can be damaged. This is why a person with sickle cell disease is more likely to get infections. His or her body isn't able to defend itself properly. So, children with sickle cell disease usually take **penicillin,** a medicine that helps prevent infections. They take the medicine twice a day, every day, until they are at least five years old.

Sickle cell crises

People with sickle cell disease have periods of pain. A period of pain is called a sickle cell **crisis.** Most people find that something warm, like a hot-water bottle, helps soothe the pain. If the pain is strong, many people take **pain relievers** to get rid of it.

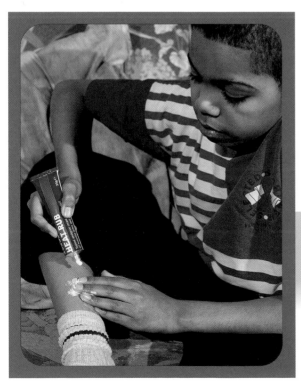

Some children find that rubbing medicated cream on the sore part of their body helps ease the pain.

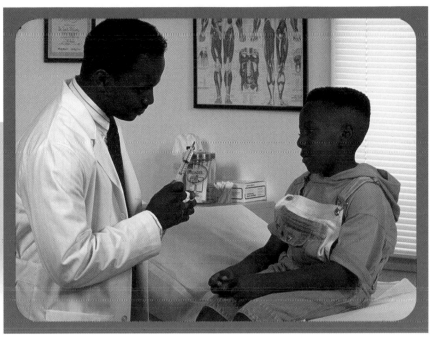

You might not like the idea of vaccinations, but they help protect you from diseases. For a friend who has sickle cell disease, vaccinations are even more important.

Vaccinations

Shots called **vaccinations** protect people from serious sicknesses like measles and mumps. Children in the United States get vaccinations for about nine different illnesses before they start school. There are also vaccinations for other diseases that can be given to help keep children from getting sick.

It's important for everyone to have vaccinations. But it's even more important for children with sickle cell disease. They are more likely to get very ill if they get sick. A child with sickle cell disease will need all the same vaccinations as any other child. However, he or she may also get some extra ones to make sure they are protected from getting many kinds of sicknesses.

Taking folic acid is one thing people can do to help with the symptoms of sickle cell disease.

Other treatments

Many children with sickle cell disease suffer from **anemia.** Their bodies need help making more **red blood cells.** People with sickle cell disease sometimes take a kind of vitamin called **folic acid.** It is found in many fruits and vegetables. Folic acid helps your body make new blood cells. These cells replace the old ones that are always wearing out. Folic acid can be taken as a liquid or a pill. Most children with sickle cell disease take folic acid every day. This helps their bodies make enough red blood cells.

Some children with sickle cell disease need blood **transfusions.** In a blood transfusion, new, healthy blood is put into a person's body to replace the person's unhealthy blood. For people with sickle cell disease, blood transfusions increase the amount of normal **hemoglobin** in their blood. People who often have problems with **blood vessel** blockage to the brain or heart might need to have transfusions every month.

Bone marrow transplants

Inside many of your bones is a soft, spongy substance called **bone marrow.** Bone marrow is sort of like a thick jelly. Its job is to make blood cells.

Doctors have found that bone marrow **transplants** can sometimes cure sickle cell disease. In a bone marrow transplant, the bone marrow of a healthy person is put into the bones of a person with sickle cell disease. A bone marrow transplant allows the body of a person with sickle cell disease to make healthy blood cells instead of sickle cells.

But not many people with sickle cell disease can get transplants because they are difficult for doctors to do. They also cost a lot of money and the patient needs to be in the hospital for a long time. And transplants don't always work. When they do, however, the new bone marrow can help make new, healthy blood cells for a person with sickle cell disease.

Often the bone marrow for a transplant comes from the brother or sister of a person with sickle cell disease.

Classmates with Sickle Cell Disease

Most children with sickle cell disease can join in all the usual school activities. However, they may have to miss school sometimes. Classmates with sickle cell disease will have to visit their doctors for regular checkups to make sure they're staying healthy and growing properly.

A classmate might also miss school because of a sickle cell **crisis.** It's very hard for a student to concentrate on schoolwork when he or she is in pain. If the pain is very bad, your classmate may need to stay home and rest or visit the doctor. Students with sickle cell disease might also have to miss school to have blood **transfusions.**

Staying indoors

Sometimes a friend with sickle cell disease might not go outside for recess. If it's very cold outside, he or she might need to stay indoors where it's warm. This is because cold weather can cause them to have a crisis. You might want to stay inside with your friend and play games or read books together.

Students with sickle cell disease work hard to keep up with schoolwork when they miss school.

Many different things can bring on a crisis for a classmate who has sickle cell disease. These include having an **infection,** being thirsty, getting very excited, and being in cold weather. Even getting a bump or a bruise can sometimes cause a crisis. Some of your classmates can tell ahead of time that they are about to have a crisis. They may feel thirsty, or they may feel more cranky or tired than usual.

Children with sickle cell disease need to drink water often to keep from becoming dehydrated.

During the school day

Classmates with sickle cell disease need to drink water or juice often during the school day. If they don't drink enough liquid, they could become dehydrated. Being dehydrated can bring on a crisis. Having to drink a lot means a friend with sickle cell disease will need to go to the bathroom more often. It's easier if he or she doesn't always have to ask the teacher to be excused every time. So you might notice your friend leaving the classroom from time to time.

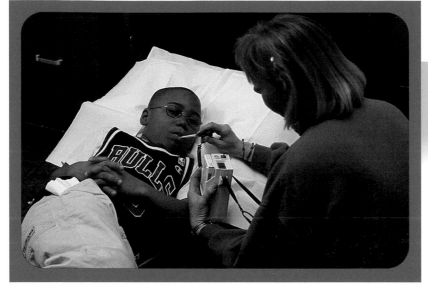

If a classmate with sickle cell disease is feeling tired, he might need to rest in the nurse's office.

Classmates with sickle cell disease might need to keep medicines, such as **pain relievers,** at school. That way they can take them if they have pain during the school day. Most of the time, a classmate's medicine is kept in the school nurse's office. A classmate might also need a quiet place to rest if he or she is feeling very tired. So you might notice a friend with sickle cell disease going to the nurse's office for a while during the day.

A classmate with sickle cell disease may miss a math or spelling test because he or she is resting in the nurse's office because of a **crisis.** Usually that's not a big problem. He or she can probably catch up. But it's harder for a classmate to keep up with schoolwork if he or she misses a lot of school days. If a classmate has to be in the hospital, many hospitals have teachers that can help him or her keep up with schoolwork.

Sports and exercise

Exercise is good for everyone, including people with sickle cell disease. Just because a classmate has sickle cell disease doesn't mean that he or she can't play games or sports. However, classmates with sickle cell disease do have to be careful playing in cold or wet weather. They have to be sure to wear warm clothing because getting chilled can cause a crisis. When a person is cold, **blood vessels** near their skin get smaller. This squeezes the blood **cells** closer together. Sickle cells are then more likely to get stuck in the blood vessels and cause a crisis.

Classmates with sickle cell disease should swim only if the water is warm. A heated, indoor pool is usually warm enough. They also must be sure to keep warm after leaving the water. **Anemia** may make them feel weak, tired, or out of breath. So they may have to avoid sports or games where they run a lot.

With a little care, most children with sickle cell disease are able to do things they enjoy with their friends.

How You Can Help

Many children with sickle cell disease grow more slowly than their classmates, and other students may tease or pick on them because of their size. They might also get picked on because they spend time in the nurse's office or miss a lot of school. And some classmates might not want to be around a person with sickle cell disease because they think they could "catch" it from them.

If you see someone being teased or picked on, you should tell a teacher. If you're worried about getting into trouble with the bullies, tell the teacher when no one else is around. Sometimes it helps if a parent or teacher explains to the class what sickle cell disease is. Then your classmates will better understand the challenges that a student with sickle cell disease has to live with.

Once people know what having sickle cell disease is all about, they can help and support a friend who has it.

Sometimes friends with sickle cell disease may get upset because they get tired easily and have pain. They may get mad because they can't play as hard as their classmates can. And they might feel it's unfair that they have a disease when other children don't.

Being in pain or always feeling tired can be very hard for a person. But there are some ways you can help a friend who has sickle cell disease. Suppose you notice that your friend seems tired on the playground at recess. You can remind him or her to take a break and rest. Your friend will be more likely to rest if you join him or her.

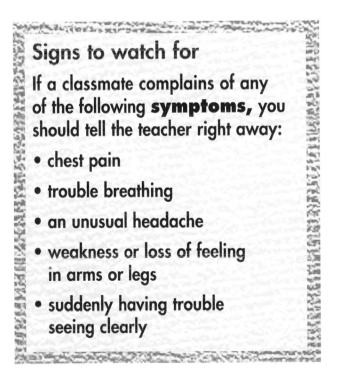

Signs to watch for

If a classmate complains of any of the following **symptoms,** you should tell the teacher right away:

- chest pain
- trouble breathing
- an unusual headache
- weakness or loss of feeling in arms or legs
- suddenly having trouble seeing clearly

Visiting a Friend with Sickle Cell Disease

A friend with sickle cell disease has to take good care of his or her health. Staying healthy will help lessen the **symptoms** of the disease. It can also help your friend avoid having a sickle cell **crisis.**

One of the things you might notice when visiting a friend's house who has sickle cell disease is that they make sure to eat properly. A balanced diet, including lots of fruits and vegetables, helps your friend's body fight off **infections.** Your friend will probably also drink lots of water or juice to keep from becoming dehydrated. A healthy after-school snack of juice or fruit can help both of you stay healthy.

Unless you spend the night at your friend's house, you might not see him or her taking **folic acid.** Most children take the vitamin only once a day in the morning.

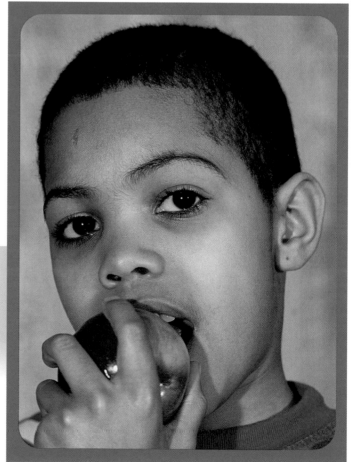

Eating plenty of healthy foods can help a child with sickle cell disease feel better.

If a friend with sickle cell disease can't play outside in cold weather, you can enjoy making artwork or other indoor activities.

Staying warm

Another thing your friend has to be careful about is staying warm. Children with sickle cell disease should try not to let themselves get cold. If they get very cold, it's hard for them to get warm again. It might also cause a sickle cell crisis. Your friend might get a little bit annoyed when a parent reminds him or her to put on a hat and gloves. But he or she knows how important it is to do things that help avoid a crisis.

If it's too cold for your friend to play outdoors, you can always find fun things to do inside. You might play checkers or cards. Or you might play a video game or watch a movie together. Spending time with your friend and doing things you both enjoy is the most important thing.

23

A sickle cell crisis might keep your friend home from a planned activity, but you can find other fun things to do together instead.

Unexpected crises

Sometimes your friend's **condition** might keep him or her from a planned activity. Suppose you have planned to go to the zoo with your friend and his or her family. If your friend has a pain **crisis** that day, the family won't be able to go. Your friend might feel upset and angry because the trip was canceled. **Pain relievers** might ease your friend's pain, but by that time it might be too late to go to the zoo, so your friend might still feel upset. You can remind your friend that it's not a big deal, and you can find other things to do together. You might suggest playing a board game or putting together a jigsaw puzzle instead.

If you spend the night at your friend's house, he might need to go to bed early if he is feeling very tired or is resting from a crisis. This will help him feel better and avoid more pain.

Exercise

Everybody should get some exercise every day. This helps keep your body in shape and healthy enough to avoid getting sick. Your friend with sickle cell disease needs exercise just as much as you do. But it doesn't always have to be hard exercise. Just taking a long walk with your friend can be enough.

Having fun together

In spite of the problems they sometimes have, most children with sickle cell disease don't feel sorry for themselves. Your friend doesn't want you to feel sorry for him or her either. Your friend just wants to enjoy spending time with you and other friends.

Your friend with sickle cell disease might tire easily because they have **anemia.** So it's important that he or she doesn't overdo it. You might need to remind your friend to take a break while you're playing and drink some water or juice. That way you can help your friend avoid a crisis.

Sickle cell disease doesn't have to get in the way of having fun and achieving goals.

Sickle Cell Success Stories

Walter Elwood Brandon was one of four children. All of the children in his family had sickle cell disease. Many times all four of them were ill at the same time. Because of this, the family had huge medical bills. Walter survived, but because doctors didn't know much about the disease then, the other children died from sickle cell disease before they grew up. As an adult, Walter was one of the people who started the Sickle Cell Disease Association of America (SCDAA) in 1971. He has written a book about his life and also speaks to groups of people about the disease.

In 1976, the Sickle Cell Disease Association of America (SCDAA) picked its first National Poster Child. The organization has continued to choose a poster child every year since then. The poster child helps other children learn about sickle cell disease. He or she also serves as a role model for other children with the disease.

Tionne Watkins was **diagnosed** with sickle cell disease when she was seven years old. But that didn't stop her from going after her dream of being a singer. Many people now know her as T-Boz from the group TLC. When the group went on tour in 1992, few people knew that she suffered from sickle cell disease. Traveling and performing shows almost every night was difficult for her. The other group members knew that she was in pain before and after their shows. One night Tionne finally collapsed. She ended up being in the hospital for two weeks. After she got out of the hospital, she realized she had to take better care of herself. She gets more rest now and makes sure she eats a healthy diet. She has worked with the Sickle Cell Disease Association of America to help teach people about the disease.

One in twelve African Americans has **sickle cell trait.** Reverend Jesse Jackson is one of those people. In 1968 he became very ill and was rushed to the hospital. Blood tests showed that Reverend Jackson had sickle cell trait, but that was not the cause of his illness.

Learning More about Sickle Cell Disease

If you have a friend with sickle cell disease, accept them and like them for being themselves. Remember, sickle cell disease isn't something your friend should be ashamed or embarrassed about.

If you want to learn more about sickle cell disease, many groups and organizations offer information about it. Going through this information with parents and teachers can help you better understand the causes, treatments, and **symptoms** of sickle cell disease.

Sickle Cell Disease Association of America (SSDAA)
200 Corporate Pointe, Suite 495
Culver City, CA 90230
310-216-6363

American Sickle Cell Anemia Association
10300 Carnegie Avenue
Cleveland Clinic/East Office Building
Cleveland, OH 44106
216-229-8600

Center for Sickle Cell Disease
Howard University
2121 Georgia Avenue NW
Washington, D.C. 20059
202-806-7930

National Association for Sickle Cell Disease
3345 Wilshire Boulevard, Suite 1106
Los Angeles, CA 90010
800-421-8453

The Sickle Cell Information Center
P.O. Box 109
Grady Memorial Hospital
80 Butler Street SE
Atlanta, GA 30303
404-616-3572

Glossary

anemia   condition in which a person's body does not have enough red blood cells or hemoglobin. People with anemia are often tired because their bodies aren't getting enough oxygen.

blood vessel   tiny tube through which blood travels in your body

bone marrow   soft, spongy material inside some bones that makes new blood cells

carrier   term used to refer to a person who has sickle cell trait

cell   tiny, living building block that makes up all the parts of a living thing

condition   health problem that a person has for a long time, perhaps for all of his or her life

crisis   period of pain caused when sickle cells block the flow of blood to a part of the body. The word crises means more than one crisis.

diagnose   to recognize what illness or condition a person has

folic acid   type of vitamin that helps the body make red blood cells

gene   tiny unit inherited from parents that controls a particular characteristic of a person

hemoglobin   substance in red blood cells that carries oxygen to cells in the body

immune system   parts of the body, including organs and cells, that work together to defend it from infection and fight off sickness

infection   sickness caused by germs entering the body

inherited   received from one's parents. The genes for sickle cell disease and other characteristics are inherited.

pain reliever   medicine that gets rid of pain

penicillin   medicine that can help keep a person from getting infections

red blood cell   type of blood cell that contains hemoglobin and carries oxygen to other body cells

sickle cell trait   condition that occurs when a person inherits one sickle cell gene and one normal gene from their parents

symptom   change in the body that is a sign of a health problem; the effect an illness or condition has on the body

transfusion   replacing the unhealthy blood in a person with new, healthy blood

transplant   to move part of one person's body to another person's body through surgery

vaccination   shot that keeps a person from getting a sickness

More Books to Read

Gold, Susan Dudley. *Sickle Cell Disease*. Berkeley Heights, NJ: Enslow Publishers, 2001.

Gordon, Melanie. *Let's Talk about Sickle Cell Anemia*. New York: PowerKids Press, 2000.

Silverstein, Alvin, Virginia Silverstein and Laura Silverstein Nunn. *Sickle Cell Anemia*. Berkeley Heights, NJ: Enslow Publishers, 1997.

Index